Perspectives on the
Real War

Perspectives on the Real War

◆

Essays of a Human Condition in Crisis

Tony A Harris, Jr.

iUniverse, Inc.

New York Lincoln Shanghai

Perspectives on the Real War
Essays of a Human Condition in Crisis

iUniverse books may be ordered through booksellers or by contacting:

iUniverse
2021 Pine Lake Road, Suite 100
Lincoln, NE 68512
www.iuniverse.com
1-800-Authors (1-800-288-4677)

ISBN-13: 978-0-595-38038-1 (pbk)
ISBN-13: 978-0-595-82408-3 (ebk)
ISBN-10: 0-595-38038-7 (pbk)
ISBN-10: 0-595-82408-0 (ebk)

Printed in the United States of America

I dedicate this work to El Shaddai (The Almighty God) who by His grace and mercy entrusted me with this writing gift and message for His people. To My Lord and Savior Jesus Christ who by His awesome sacrifice made it possible for me to live fully and freely and to the precious Holy Spirit who convicts me, corrects me and guides my every move.

To the children of Richmond Public Schools in Richmond, Va. (particularly those of the Richmond Alternative Program,) for you have been my inspiration. I am also thankful for my experiences at The Samuel Dewitt Proctor School of Theology at Virginia Union University where I currently attend and perfect the fusion of faith and social justice.

I am finally thankful for the two dedicated and loving women in my life whom God has used to motivate me; to allow the best of me to emerge: my beloved mother, Carolyn Williams and my precious wife Najiyyah Brooks Harris.

Contents

Foreword

In 1904, W. E. B. DuBois prophesied that the "problem of the 20th century would be the problem of the color line." Now, well into the 21st century it appears that Americans—on both sides of the color line—continue to struggle with issues of race and the extent to which race is all too often a determinant of destiny.

A young voice of this new century is that of Tony A Harris, Jr., born in the latter years of the last century, but whose mark will be made in this one. In the essays of this volume, the reader will hear the voice of a young African American who is passionately concerned about where we are and where we are going. He is worried about African American life and some of the obstacles that prevent blacks from achieving our God-given potential. He is worried about the spiritual and mental malaise that seems to hover in too many places over our people, young and old.

These essays challenge us to move from a lethargy and crippling cynicism evidenced in far too many areas of African American life to levels of achievement that characterized the lives of our forebears, who, having less, left an inestimable legacy on which we can build.

It is my hope that those who read these essays will gain much through them and thereby fulfill the vision that inspires them.

Dr. Samuel K. Roberts

Anne Borden and E. Hervey Evans
Professor of Theology and Ethics
Union Theological Seminary/
Presbyterian School of Christian Education

Author of: *In the Path of Virtue: the African American Moral Tradition* (1999) and *African American Christian Ethics* (2001), both published by The Pilgrim Press, Cleveland.

Preface: A Need to Take Heed

o o o o o o o o o o o o o o o o o o o o o o o o o o o o o o o o o o o o

*It is impossible to accurately determine **where we are going** without doing two things: We must first take a meticulous inventory of **where we have been** and secondly, honestly assess **where we are**. It is only here in the culmination of these two truths do we find the audacity to chart a dream of progress not mired in child-like fantasy but immersed in realism, faith, and conviction.*

—Tony Avon Harris, Jr.

There is a dilemma in all of America, Black America in particular and the dilemma is that we have planted *unproductive seeds*. The ground has proven to be infertile, for it has been the victim of a land undernourished. The weather has been formidable and unforgiving while our planting tools have been both antiquated and remedial at best. What I am talking about are the issues concerning our children and the disenfranchised; their quest for justice represents the battleground for the *next* generation of *America*. We are often unnerved by the offspring that we ourselves have produced. We look upon them in most circles with a total lack of compassion. Our disdain and pessimism are evident as we proclaim that we do not understand their ways. However, we do not have any reason to be upset with our harvest because it has direct correlation with the seeds we have planted. Our youth, (particularly those who are African American) mirror our indifference, our complacency, our latent anger and frustration, our disunity, our vices and moral deficiencies. They mirror our attitudes of helplessness concerning our plight on this North American continent. The truth of the matter is that our children did not come up with these attributes *independently*, but we passed these wonderful personality flaws on to them. It is now our duty to *fertilize* the soil, to *plant* better seeds and to *give both life sustaining "water and sunlight,"*—then we will be pleased (and at the same time amazed) at the *fruit* that is produced.

We must take a more active parenting role in the lives of young Americans. We must take a more inclusive role in the lives for all Americans. We must seek to aid not only our biological children and those belonging to our families, but all children. We all belong to each other. We must reach back and pull them forward now, for they will be the ones who will eventually carry us. It is all too common now particularly in our African American communities, that we have become a generation of "fatherless" children. We have become a nation of children rearing children, or even worse children rearing themselves. This trend has caused generational animosity between both parent and child played out in all too familiar conversation. Can you hear the child who almost fully grown proclaims to the parent *"Where were you when I needed you? You weren't there in all that I went through. Didn't you care? Well if you don't care, I DON'T CARE!"* Anyone who has lived to hear this dialogue knows that it isn't true, the children *do care*. The same can be said about the misplaced, displaced and disenfranchised, they do care. However, the rift between the privileged and the underprivileged as well as that of the proverbial father and child can never be underestimated. The bond that *never was* will have long lasting effects. Because of severed relationships the treasures of the past will never find their passport into the present. The question we must now ask ourselves is "what will tomorrow look like as a result?"

We must understand that we have more responsibility for shaping tomorrow than we think *because we shape the next generation today.* It is on **this day** that we set the course for the next fifty years; what will our legacy be to our children? If you pay attention to pop culture, have spent any time in a school or even take the time to watch BET or MTV; you understand full well that the battle lines have already been drawn and the task ahead is an arduous one. As a matter of fact we are already in retreat and some would rather leave our young behind as *casualties of war.* Yet I urge you not to retreat but to *regroup*, I urge us all to be unified again. We don't have to be **uniform to be unified**. We don't all have to attack at the same time or with the same weaponry; however, we should all attack with the same deliberateness and synchronicity in heart, mind, and soul as to secure total victory. Today I urge all of America to *wake up,* and I urge African Americans to *step up.* The whole world and all of creation for that matter groans in expectation, waiting to see *what we will become.* It is time for the youth of African Americans (and the youth of all America) to come into themselves and be who they were called to be. It is also time for the disenfranchised, disadvantaged, and oppressed to be liberated and empowered. Our country so desperately needs for it to happen, the world is waiting for it to happen and God has ordained that it shall happen. Today is the day.

Amen...

Article 1:
The Need for Mobilization

"Let the word go forth from this time and place, to friend and foe alike, that the torch has been passed to a new generation of Americans.."

> —*John F. Kennedy, 1/19/1961*

My eyes grow weary, weighted with the heaviness that comes from holding back my bucket load of tears. As I survey this red, white, and blue panorama I ask myself the question that I assume many African Americans and other minorities have asked, "Is this *truly* my country?" I ask myself often, "Is this the *Land of the Free* and the *Home of the Brave?*" "Is this a land that *flows with milk and honey*" I ask myself, "and if so where does my economic empowerment and opportunity lie?" When I think of America, this melting pot, this grandiose cauldron of socio-political and economic landscape, I sometimes cry. I don't necessarily cry tears of joy, but various streams of tears. I cry tears of sadness, tears of sorrows, tears of heartache, and tears of pain. Then there are tears of frustration and tears of anger, and even tears of fear. There is a fear that maybe, just maybe this country wasn't made for me—doesn't apply to me, and it's dream illusive to me. My brothers and some sisters, the majority of which are African American die in America's streets everyday. They fall dead in the gutters and alleys; disillusioned, disappointed, disadvantaged, disenfranchised, disserviced, and disregarded.

Something must be done for my brothers and sisters, and I; something has got to give and *not us* because we *have already given everything we had*. We have *given in*, and *given up*; we have even allowed ourselves to be *given over* to anyone or anything that would to exploit us. Almost four hundred some odd years after the birth of this nation in Jamestown (1607;) some one hundred and forty years after this nation's own Civil War that divided so deeply, and forty one years after this nation's so called civil revival in1964 we still find that this nation has a lot of work to do in area of race, racial equality and brotherhood. We all have a long way to go in the efforts to achieve a most basic harmony between all of us who live on this soil and share in the vision of 1776.

I am reticent to admit it, but we are *still* at war. Right here on this soil we fight a fight that has been ignored, denied and swept under the rug over and over again. It isn't some material or interpersonal struggle such as a Vietnam, but rather a deep seeded inner personal struggle; one in which each man, woman boy or girl must decide for themselves. The stakes are much higher in this war and the casualties a little closer to home. Just take a look in the mirror and think about its victims because the war will not be fought on some foreign soil, or even on the hallowed grounds of Gettysburg. This war will be fought on the grounds of our hearts and minds. This war will continue to be fought on the more fertile and promising grounds of our children's hearts and minds. All of us, whether Black or White, Jew or Gentile, Atheist, heterosexual or homosexual have felt and will continue to feel the undercurrent, we all know that America *must* change and *change now.*

For all of us who are partakers in this Free Enterprise, we first must change ourselves, because it is with ourselves that we are at war. We are at war within ourselves and in revolt against ourselves in an effort to tear down our most crippling mindsets and handicaps. In the span of the last twenty-nine years in this nation alone (of which I have been able to term my life,) we have experienced a severe social, moral and political debacle; our progress has been stagnated by a loss of identity, loss of pride, loss of hope, and loss (in my opinion) of true leadership. We as the people—particularly the minority,—have been stripped of both resources and support and at the same time refused to be of any resource or support to anyone but ourselves. We as a people (particularly but not exclusively African Americans) have fallen victim to the revolving door of generational underachievement. Our voices have gone largely unheard, that is until *TODAY.* Today we begin to march again, march onward to liberty, self-determination, and destiny. Today I call all of America to arms; it is time to move—to be on the move!

Do you see what I see? We have our differences in such a diverse nation yet there are some things that I'm sure can be generalized to many segments of our society. My major area of experience and concern is urban America. That is not to say that there are not other problems across the nation (we all know that there are,) yet I have seen the lights flicker in their souls and heard their voices. Do you not hear the screams of our young people across this nation, these young Nubian princes and princesses; of which, will one day be our kings and queens? Have you taken the time to hear the voice of the sixteen-year-old boy who is the *only* man of his house? The voice of a youngster who must make the choice between school and home—whether to feed his mind with National and State Standards of Learning or *feed* his family with the fruits gained by illegal activity. The truth is that McDonalds won't pay his family's bills *even if they did* hire him, and so he goes with the best opportunity that he thinks will satisfy the insatiable yet corrupted desires of his community. The community will hire him, and their pay off is adequate and immediate. These pay-offs take on the form of drugs or prostitution and I know and you know that these are wrong, but what is *wrong* with him trying to feed his family? Who has offered him a feasible solution, which will make sure his family has health care and food, and clothes, and books, and paper, and toiletries? There are no simple answers. The same is the case for the fifteen-year-old girl whose father has absented himself from her life spiritually, emotionally and/or physically, a long time ago. All she wanted was validation, legitimacy and affirmation; she wanted the same thing we do which is someone to hold us and let us know that we are priceless in the midst of this world's many pleasures. She made a very costly yet common mistake in our society; she sought deliverance in the wrong thing and now she carries a seed inside of her to which she will pass on her every fear, and doubt, and insecurity. She will pass on her poverty and a paradigm of hindrance that would make it hard for anything to grow.

What chances do our children have, what chances do people who live such as these have? Have you ever looked into their eyes; do you recognize their glassy defeated stare trapped behind their hard face of reality? Can you see them as you ride down their streets? Do you even ride down their streets? My conjecture is that you don't, most of us don't. America has made the habit of either moving the problem, or *moving away* from the problem; it has become a situation of *"Out of sight, out of mind."* For these children and for others who find themselves in the "inner city," there is no economic and social prosperity and there are no amber waves of grain because their soil is *highly infertile*. They will never reach the top of a "purple mountain's majesty" because they are confined to the black mountain's valley of despairs.

When I close my eyes at night, I see their faces with their watery eyes and outstretched hands. Who will stand in the gap for them, who will protect the *gems of tomorrow* today? Who will reconnect the disconnected? Who will sing to them "We Shall Overcome!" in a language that all can understand? Who will not only *tell* the marginalized of America that "they are somebody," but also show them that they are somebody? In the case of our children, have we not forgotten that

"A child shall lead us?" How else can America propel into tomorrow unless our "sons and daughters prophesy and dream dreams?" Our young people in many instances do not even dream of *tomorrow* anymore because of the nightmares they face *today*. I wonder often, where would I be as an African American, (where would America be, period) if Martin Luther King hadn't dreamed? Where would I be if Carver, Malik Shabazz, Martin Delaney, or Dubois hadn't dreamed? What if the likes of a Sammy Davis, a Stevie Wonder, or a Langston Hughes had not followed their dreams? I'm sure that women and men of all walks of life can appreciate the R.E.M. induced cinematography spawned from the likes of a Maya Angelou, or a Zora Neale Hurston; Oprah Winfrey and Condoleezza Rice. These people allowed their dreams to fuel and empower them. We must give our young people the power to possess tomorrow, TODAY. We must foster a world for them that surpasses their most common boundaries. We must inspire them and allow them to follow their dreams. If Kobe Bryant and La Bron James do not have boundaries, why should our children? Eyes have yet to see and ears yet to hear, minds have yet to conceptualize the things that God has planned for each and everyone of them before they were born. We've put a box around our babies when we should be the ones helping them break out of the box. We need to give them wings. They need wings to both soar over poverty and fly far above the valley of depression. They'll need wings to circumvent the overt and covert racism that still runs rampant in some areas of the country. These wings will allow them the opportunity to rise above the stereotypes and labels that are placed on them. The stereotypes and labels so irresponsibly portrayed in some of the musical art forms that many of our young people so religiously subscribe. My heart has grieved at times when I have watched (and I do watch) a Black Entertainment Television or a Music Television. There was a time when both of these stations had wonderful family programs to augment the music videos, but now they exploit and abuse their young viewership by inundating their minds with images and values that are inconsistent with those *we say* we want them to exhibit. What we have done is fallen asleep "at the wheel." We have not looked out for the best interest of our babies, or each other for that matter. We have been self-serving and derelict in our duties and we are now beginning to pay for it.

Now I know that there are critics who will not agree with my position. There are some who will say that we *have* given our young people wings and that today's America (and all who live within her borders) flies higher than she has ever flown before. Some will argue that this new generation has enjoyed far more privilege than we could've ever hoped to enjoy, and to those critics I would say; "You are right." However, I would also say (and most of us know this to be true) that at this very moment in time we **could and should** be flying much higher. What is undeniable is that given all of the resources that we have-individually, and collectively—we really ought to be ashamed of ourselves. I also know that everyone doesn't function at "on or below the poverty line" and that everyone doesn't live in a ghetto. Nor are we all the products of single parent homes, or on welfare, in a gang or pregnant; however too many of us are. Until we start taking more of a vested interest in each other, we will not succeed. Until Americans are concerned about more than the people and agendas within their "inner circle," we can't succeed. Until the majority in America can get on the bandwagon and be of assistance to the minority: their African American, Hispanic, and Native Americans can expect to exist in a state of *"would have been, should have been and could have been."* Some of us have been misled to believe that we have arrived just because a few of us have arrived, but until *all of us* can raise our hands in victory, *we all* have a long way to go. We mustn't be lulled into premature celebration because of a *slice* of the pie when the *whole* pie is ours.

We have become dangerously rotund with our own success. I use the following analogy to fully illustrate the situation: One thanksgiving a child ate way too much, there was nothing outside of his reach as he continually stuffed every item on the dinner table unto his plate and then into his mouth. It wasn't long after that the young man began to become sleepy and within minutes he was fast asleep. He slept so long and hard that he missed dessert, when he woke up all of the dessert (his favorite) along with all of his relatives was gone. He stared endlessly at the table, looking directly at the dessert dish when he came to the realization that he had missed his opportunity all because he'd fallen asleep. The same is true for a lot of us; we've been missing opportunities because we find ourselves "sleep on the job." In an effort to compensate for all the food we've eaten, and the energy that must be used to digest it—our bodies have shut down, (kind of like cutting off all the lights in the house to save electricity.) This shut down, which is actually the body's way of diverting all of its energy to digestion, has in turn induced sleepiness. The body doesn't have energy to run itself because it uses it all to compensate for the body's *over consumption*. This is why a lot of us get sleepy after the big meal, and perhaps in a figurative sense—it is why we are "sleeping giants." We are so busy consuming and taking, that we don't have the energy for anything else. And while we are sleeping, who is taking care of our husbands, and wives; who is taking care of our kids and our country? Perhaps we shouldn't be surprised that our children seem unaffected by a lot and that they too are asleep to the world. They are only following our example.

We can no longer share this mindset in our homes, in our communities, or in this country. We have to sound the trumpet and gather our troops together, this is a roll call: **a call to mobilization**. It is time for us to move from *where we are* to *where we were destined to be*. This is a call to fight a war for our homes, and our jobs, our families and for equality; therefore, this is a call to arms. Take up your shields, your swords, and your crosses and fight to live life. Fight to live a life more abundantly. I call on my young brothers and sisters as well as the older brothers and sisters. I call my sisters and brothers from the east as well as the north, west, and south. I call the brothers and sisters from the city, to the suburbs to the country. I call upon the rich, the impoverished, the so called educated and non-educated. Whether you consider yourself religious or atheist it makes no difference, whoever and wherever you are WAKE UP! It's time to go to war. Today I call this young nation together, understanding that the only way we're going to make a difference is if we make it together. I challenge you make this nation a better place. We are a nation in need: in need of identity, hope, moral integrity, voice, leadership, achievement and resources. This is my perspective on the real war facing this country; we are a nation in crisis.

Article 2: A Need for Identity

War (wôr) n. A state of an open, armed conflict between nations, states, or parties. Who is the enemy and what is the scope of the conflict? The question I ask is one of definition and identity. When I speak of war, I do not speak of it lightly. My contention is that there is indeed a war in America. There is a conflict rooted firmly in both economics and race that has torn us apart since this country's founding. It is a war that has unfortunately led "brother to fight against brother" and though it does not manifest itself physically as it did in 1861, the divisive nature of it can be just as easily experienced. The weapons used in this war are far more destructive, destroying not an army at a time, but a generation at a time. It is not the blood of soldiers that is spilled across our countryside but it is the soul of America that has been eviscerated.

This is a far more pressing issue than Vietnam or Korea. This war is more threatening to our way of life than both Iraq and Afghanistan because the struggle lies within. A house divided will not stand. Though the walls of the stronghold may be high and the moat surrounding it both deep and wide; it doesn't do any good if the drawbridge is let down by someone from *within* the city. Our inability to "get along" and "get along well" has left a crack in our front door, which in turn has left us vulnerable to intruders who wish to trespass upon our ground. As a nation, we must deal with this truth with the utmost immediacy. We must come to realize that the enemy is not *terrorism* abroad but economic and racial inequalities that terrorize the integrity and beauty of this country everyday. The situation has become extreme as we look at society as a whole. It has become particularly extreme for the marginalized such as African Americans as we war for a better existence. Moreover, physical revolt and fighting is not the answer—we must look to reform our hearts and minds. We require a *new* mind to fight in this *new* day.

I first want to justify this call to arms by saying that this is **not** some extremist-militant ploy to overtake the government of the United States, nor is this some message of hate and blame toward any group of people. It is a known fact that atrocities have been committed against African Americans; innocent blood has been and continues to be shed. These atrocities, however despicable and heinous, are no different than the plight of Jews across the Diaspora, nor are the stories of the Native American or Asian American (particularly during the backlashes after World War I and Vietnam conflicts) any less deplorable. They are quite simply man's failure to live in the love, harmony, and trust intended by his Creator. It is a crime that America has refused to truly apologize and fully atone for its crimes against the African American, yet it is equally criminal to assert the contention that the problems existing in African American communities are entirely the fault of injustice and oppression. It is ludicrous and even absurd to even obliquely imply that we should continue as a people on the downward spiral to oblivion because of the bigotries of only a handful. We have *"been there"* and *"done that"* so to speak and we must now change the focus of our arguments. We must fight this war on a different front, no longer being as concerned with what *has been done to us* as we are concerned with *what now will we do for ourselves.*

I believe a certain amount of introspection must take place in our communities. Those outside looking in must be more philanthropic, while at the same time those inside looking out must learn to be more self-sufficient. When we began to change our minds then we ourselves will be open to change. The body follows the mind, even after the body has aged and withered—an acute mind can continue to be strong. In my own African American community, we must begin to re-orient our brothers and sisters to use their minds. The prowess of the African American lies not in our mouths, or fists, or any other physical acumen, but it lies in our minds. But we don't use our minds to the degree that we could or should all because we have lost the notion of who we were and who we are; we have lost a sense of identity:

Who am *I?*
What is my *D*estiny?
What am I *ENTIT*led to?
Wh*Y* is all of this important?

Of these five questions embedded in identity I start with the last, which asks the question: "Why is all of this important?" The answer can be found in one of my favorite stories entitled *The Ugly Duckling*. There was a duck born different from the others. His differences were not something appreciated, but rather they became the object of ridicule and ostracism. Then one day he came across a creature that looked like him, it was a creature of beauty and majesty and it wasn't a duck at all it was a swan. Now the *Ugly Duckling* had a roadmap to what he was to become. He had renewed spirit and confidence, and was able *to fly*. The point is quite clear that knowing who you are is the first step to being able to fly. There is however, another point intimated in this story—it is that one must first *be shown* who they are, given an example of who are; presumably by one who *has already* traveled their path. This is where we find America today. A young generation unsure of the totality of who they are and even worse, no examples to show them the way. They then fall prey to the capricious and unsteady influences of pop culture and the rest is as they say, history. When everybody and everything *tells* you who you are and you believe it then what you become *is a counterfeit something else*. Knowing "who you are" is an integral component in how you perceive yourself, equally so in how others perceive you. A life is transformed when the realization of who one truly is becomes apparent. What you will tolerate, the pride you take in yourself, the heights you believe yourself to be able to attain-these are all a function of identity. In the case of African American youth (and youth in general,) too many of the wrong people have told them who they are. Too many of them are walking around amongst ducks; they are being *quacked down* and ridiculed here on the ground when their place is in the air as a swan. This is a truth of all America but particularly for our young people in the African American Community: *OUR DESTINY IS MUCH GREATER AND OUR ENTITLEMENT LARGER, ALL BECAUSE OF WHO WE ARE.*

It is at this juncture that I must digress to address my African American brothers and sisters to clarify the delineation between *who we were* at some point in history and *who we are*. There have been too many that have made the mistake of either using slavery as the starting point in our history, or the early civilizations of Africa (Egypt, Carthage, Ghana, Songhay..) as our Golden Age and end point. Our history cannot be relegated to subordinance or servitude anymore than it can be to riches or kingdoms. They are not separate or even dichotomous histories, but they are both part of one and the same. It is the history of a people walking through the annals of time colored with both up and downs, and yet we still stand. I share this history as an African American with our youth in the hopes that it will spark a fire that causes them to burn an eternal flame. However, I and we also share this story with the larger American community and the world abroad because it is a story shared by every human being and every people on the face of this earth. We *still* stand, even in the midst of adversity. Let us now continue to stand against the real enemy of inequality and the real war to gain victory for all mankind.

We have all become a bit too enamored with the triune trap of *Money, Sex,* and *Power* as a means of defining ourselves. These three vices spur from very ancient and innate lusts, lusts of both our eyes and flesh and the pride of life. They have become Man's sole pursuit in life leading him down a road of emptiness, disappointment and soul destruction. Our dilemma can be summated as such: *Money* in this capitalistic free enterprise offers one all that they can see; *Sex* gives the affirmation (perverted into aggrandizement) that one never knew and finally *Power*, an illusion of influence and control that only belongs to God. All of these things are cosmetic in nature at best; exterior and temporal in nature offering very little stability and dependency. They are often facades, covering emotional bankruptcy and ineptness. They offer no real guarantees and those who partake in the roll of the dice find themselves subject to the whims of a fickle world. When they are *up* they are up but when they are *down*, they are not only down but often *out.* They are tossed to and fro like a sailboat in the wind and they are at the mercy of the storm going wherever it takes them *unless they have an anchor.* A sense of identity is your anchor reaching down deep into the sea in the midst of the wind. We must learn as well as teach our young the art of *anchoring themselves*, to have an identity that is rooted and fixed lest we blow away with winds in the population of the masses.

The central question is *"Who are we?"* or more importantly *"Who are you?"* Before we can have a national identity there must be individual identity. I'm not talking about fragmentation, but a more holistic approach to the American Dream. This is an approach where I understand that before my family can be whole I must be whole; where I understand before my community can be whole my family must be whole. This is an approach where finally I understand that before my nation can be whole, communities must first be whole. I liken this exercise to taking any cumulative course in school such as math or language arts. You must master the elementary basics before you can move to the more advanced. However, on that same premise I do believe that our young people (who are by far more sophisticated and experienced than we were at their ages) can better understand who they are *within the context* of who we are. You see I've noticed their trend of isolationism, and their bodacious independence as well as their desire to define themselves *for themselves and by themselves*. However, I do believe that this was brought on more by necessity than their own desire.

We dropped the ball in nurturing them and we failed to give them our love. We were the ones who abdicated our responsibility to television, to teachers, to the streets and to the juvenile justice system. Our children only did what was natural by any evolutionary perspective: they adapted to the void and learned to survive without us. And so now we must **earn** the right of guardianship, we must **regain** both their trust and respect, we must now **seek** forgiveness, we must come *alongside* them and as they *allow* us, mentor them into adulthood.

The fact of the matter is that as well as our youth have adapted, (particularly our underprivileged and inner city youth) they can never gain the full perspective of who they are and who they were meant to be without a real sense of who we were, and where we've been. It's like picking up a book and starting to read smack dab in the middle of it, right as the plot begins to thicken. You might deem it a good book and you might even find that you half way understand what has taken place; however it is much easier, and you will understand much better if you simply provide the background information and start from the beginning. This is the gift of unbiased, openly critiqued, and debatable history. I believe that by helping young people to fully understand whom we are as a collective people—including both a thorough and truthful perspective of were we have been—then we could help them to better define themselves. We will help them to not only define themselves apart from us but in relation to us as well. This act will do wonders to bridge the intergenerational gaps that exist in this country. We often wonder why we don't see eye to eye with each other, and that's because we fail to see each other in another's shoes.

Once again, I contend that this trend isn't just an issue rooted in my African American context, but one seen in much larger proportion in the American context. It is our young who are going to determine where we shall go as a nation in the immediate future, and they who of course will have "final say" in laying the groundwork for the destinies of future generations. Many of us who rear and mentor them will be either elderly or eventually dead. Our impact is on today more so than tomorrow. However, we are not absolved from our responsibility to give insightful and inspiring input. Let us not be derelict in our duties to *prepare our birds for flight*. We can't make them flap their wings, but we should have fed them and taken care of them (up to the appointed age) before we kicked them out of the nest. For at least a generation in my own community, (and perhaps two) I have seen the succeeding generation grow up without the benefits and treasures gained by their elders despite making more monetary strides. They have not known the mistakes and triumphs of history, they do not know the plight of the preceding generation. Instead of starting life with a "healthy trust fund" of life's experience, they start off bankrupt. They start at zero balance if they are lucky, and often they come into the world with a negative balance.

We must take a more active approach with our young people and we must have more of a hand in shaping a more positive identity. Identity comes through the teaching of history, both its triumphs and mistakes as well as its lessons learned and errors repeated. History allows us to give a better context in informing young people of who we were. It is not just the teaching of history, but the reacquainting ourselves with the beliefs that have sustained us through history. Beliefs that are deeply embedded within us, beliefs upon which lie the sole reason of the existence of an America. We are, and have always been *ONE NATION UNDER GOD*. We have forgotten many things over the course of history. Prosperity, Pluralism, Political correctness—all have shrouded our sense of identity. It is no wonder that we have lost our sense of identity as a nation because we have lost it as communities and as individuals. Many would argue, but America's *theology* has changed and this has brought a change in both America's *sociology* and *psychology*. If we look deep within our history we will find the true measuring stick of Man's identity and that was and is, his belief in God. It was *God who endowed us with certain alienable rights*, it is the *first amendment* right that a man's relationship with Him *should not be prohibited*. It was *God* who was worshipped in the very *rotunda of capital itself by some of the founding fathers* of this country and *in God that we say we trust*. God preserved us through a civil war, even to this very day. It is God who we ask *to bless America,* and to *shed His grace* on us. He is the *God of our weary years and the God of our silent years* and it is in Him that the most basic questions of identity are answered.

If we along with our young people are going to take up arms and win this fight, then we all need to know from whence we have come. To survive as a community, we must begin to see ourselves united together. The success and revitalization of our disadvantaged and disenfranchised communities benefit all involved regardless of age, color, creed, or economic station. The success of a new America can be the catalyst for success in a new world, a new world where men love their neighbors as they love themselves. If a man has not first loved himself then he cannot love others. Who can truly love themselves without first *truly knowing themselves?* We are called to greatness, not in some distant future but today. Today we reclaim our identity and in doing so have a new hope.

Article 3: A Need for Hope

o o o o o o o o o o o o o o o o o o o o o o o o o o o o o o o o o

"Ten seconds from saying I can't do this here; Ten seconds from saying man I'm through with this; Ten seconds from leaving cuz I'm confused with this and that's a half a minute from straight up losing it!"

—*Allen Harris [NEWLIFE]*

I can remember in my in 2nd or 3rd year of teaching I had a student who was gunned down on the basketball court in one of the neighborhoods surrounding the school. He couldn't have been any more than 14 or 15 years old, far too young to die such a senseless death. He was in the 7th grade and a repeat student; an occurrence all too accepted in his urban setting. He was a delightful teen full of personality and dreams but school wasn't necessarily his forte. There were many reasons for his seemed academic anemia; none of which pointed to his lack of intelligence or giftedness. He was one of those students you really hated to see do poorly; he had a wonderful disposition and so much latent potential. I went to his funeral with tears in my eyes, remembering his love for finance despite his disdain for math (math homework at least.) I remembered how he dreamed of an occupation in finance, hoping to follow in the footsteps of an elder relative. This child, while performing less than stellar in a 7th grade math class, could calculate percentage increase and decrease as well as sales tax with uncanny ease. I always felt that given a little bit of time and direction, he'd grow up to be all he wanted to be. Above all else the student had hope, and very seldom approached life with less than a smile. Though his life was short lived, I do believe he lived a fuller life than most of us do because despite his circumstance he never lost hope. I parallel this story with a story a co-worker told me about a man they knew whose life wasn't taken by someone else, but forfeited as a result of his suicide. He unlike my student was considered "successful." He had a big house and a wonderful marriage; he had the whole package. He was a man of faith who had served in the military; he was respected and supported by many people. By a freak act of violence he lost the use of his legs, and with his legs went his hope. Overtime a once happy man became embittered and depressed and he shot himself, leaving his family to pick up the pieces while asking themselves all along that driving question: Why?

What makes a man, woman, boy or girl decide that they would forfeit the gift of life itself? What makes one want to "call it quits," FOR GOOD? Why do many people seek such an *eternal* solution, when the *condition* they are facing is *temporal?* It's one thing to die naturally and it is something else to die in a random act of violence. However, it is an entirely different tragedy when one *gives* up their life volitionally. If the truth were told, this sickness called suicide isn't such an enigma at all. I don't mean to oversimplify the issue (nor am I an expert on the matter,) but I see it as a person's last effort to stop the pain; it is someone's last *gamble* for a better situation (or at least a reprieve on the other side.) The person desires to stop the discomfort so desperately that they have lost their will, their *hope* to live. It is a very unfortunate occurrence because in many cases, the suicide could have been averted. If we had just listened to (and taken seriously) both the subtle and not so subtle cries for help; if we had only taken time from our busy schedules and been a little more receptive to our loved ones in their time of need, then perhaps we could have saved their lives.

Now there are some of us who would like to believe that this isn't a problem pertaining to them or anyone they know for that matter; and if that is indeed the case then they find themselves a part of a very privileged minority. However, I implore them along with the rest of us in America to pay very close attention to this matter, as it is an everyday reality for many of us. The life you save could very well be someone you hold most dear, at any rate a life is something that we really can't afford to *lose.* The biggest myth is that only weak people commit suicide, but I can personally attest that *everyday* **strong** people contemplate death by suicide. There have been many dark nights in my life when I earnestly and fervently prayed for death. I can remember mornings when I was deeply disappointed to wake up and see another day. There have been seasons in my life when I'd lost all desire to live, and all **hope** for a better day. I watched the leaves fall and die in the winter and empathized with them, never taking into consideration that the tree would bloom again in the spring.

There are many who have shared in my experiences and yet, however you do not have to take our word for it. The veracity of our claims concerning suicide can be confirmed by many sources including these from the *Nation's Voice on Mental Illness* or [NAMI:]

- In 1996, more teenagers died from suicide than from cancer, heart disease, AIDS, birth defects, stroke, Pneumonia, influenza, and chronic lung disease combined.

- In 1996, suicide was the 2nd leading cause of death among college students, 3rd amongst those ages 15 to 24 and 4th for those aged 10 to14 years old.

- From 1980–1996, the suicide rate for African America males increased 105%.

And while these numbers have been on a slight decline in more recent years, suicide remains the 8th leading cause of death in the United States; it is 3rd between young people aged 15–24 years old. To be blunt my brothers and sisters, our young people have lost hope. They have lost interest in life, they have lost all energy; they have lost all motivation to keep on moving. *They feel worthless and even if they've never said it* their behaviors *scream it* out loud. Our young people—along with many other marginalized people—are both angry and sad at the same time; they are abusing drugs, they are abusing alcohol, they are abusing themselves and being misused sexually. They are quite simply hurting. They are hurting so much that the only thing that they really know how to do is to continue to hurt themselves. They are doing poor in school, they are living poorer at home; their souls and their lives are spiritually impoverished. These problems begin to persist in a cyclical fashion; each one perpetuating the other until they consume and engulf the individual, compounding generational misery upon generation misery. They allow their lives to **EXPIRE** because no one ever took the time or gave them reason to be **INSPIRED**. Even if they don't commit the physical act of suicide they spiritually and mentally withdraw from life every single day, bringing new meaning to the phrase *"killing me softly."* But I pause at this moment to say that the maladies that affect this young nation aren't terminal. I pause at this moment to proclaim that we can turn back the sands of the hourglass. We can reverse the trend, and we can raise the "dead." Our young nation can be revived; they can be *resurrected or re-erected.* Our young people will learn to stand on their own two feet again and they will no longer stumble. They will no longer fall but they will stand again. Our babies (particularly our African American babies) may not be where we want or need them to be, they may be underachieving at the moment but they can get up from their fallen state. All our children—and anyone else for that matter—need is for someone to stick their hand out, not a pointed finger but an outstretched arm and a helping hand, both of which are preceded by an open heart and an open mind. Our young people need to be assured that we will support them whether they look like us or not; whether they act like us or not; and most importantly whether they think like us or not. We may not always agree with them, or even condone all of their activities but we should always be supportive of them. We should always *speak life in them* and not allow death to consume them. As an African American, I realize that we don't have to be **uniform in thought** in order to be **unified as a race.** If we could only grasp the concept of unity as a race, then we would not retrogress in the quagmire of depravity that we do from time to time. If America understood this as a nation we wouldn't have to fight the same conflicts we've fought since the Civil War and Reconstruction, not to mention the struggles we have abroad with other nations. We might help to police the world, but I do not believe that we should do it in manner that is more consistent with martial law. We are all in this together. If we could only fight for our young people as ardently and arduously as we fight with them. They need to know that they can achieve, and on their own terms. We as a people have come a mighty long way, we as a nation have really come through some adversity, and yet I believe our best days are yet to come. I do not believe in America because we are so special, but because our children are so special. They will benefit from the mistakes of our past, as well as from our triumph. There are jobs for them to have (or create,) businesses for them to run, families to raise and a nation to lead. There are records for them to set and break as well as new battles for them to fight and win. They have talents within themselves that are waiting to be unveiled; they have their own dreams to fulfill (and so we can not vicariously fulfill ours through them,) and their own heights to achieve if only they can believe. If only they had ***HOPE***, if we only did *more to instill* that hope in them. If they could live through the "night" in their lives, they would wake to know the joy in the morning. Whatever you do as you are reading this book never allow yourself or anyone you know to lose hope; if a man or woman loses hope then they have truly lost indeed. You must know that optimism is just as infectious as pessimism; as long as you have hope no one around you should be devoid of it. If you have met anyone (particularly our young) who has **lost** hope, you should do everything in your power to help them **find** it again. Look into their bright and beautiful eyes and allow them to know that they diamonds in the rough. Look into their eyes to see the visions of tomorrow. Realize that the visions of tomorrow are built upon today and so we must preserve today in order to make it to tomorrow. Don't let our kids give up in the midst of the process, particularly in urban African American communities where dropout and incarceration rates rival if not exceed those of college entry rates. It is the *process* that changes the caterpillar to a butterfly, the *process* that changes coal into diamonds, the *process* that changes grapes into wine, and the *process* that refines fine metals such as silver or gold to the degree that one could see their reflection in them. If the generations to come can remain hopeful in the midst of their process then the reflection that they see will eventually be one majesty, power, and beauty. The image that they see will be perfection reminiscent of the Creator who is the origin of both mankind and the attributes present within them. Give our young people hope and intervene before they commit emotional, physical, and spiritual suicide. Intervene in the lives of our young before they abort their promise and purpose, for both of which there is no replacement.

Article 4:
The Need for Moral Integrity

"Moral principals have lost their distinctiveness. For modern man, absolute right and wrong are a matter of what the majority is doing. Right and wrong are relative to likes and dislikes and the customs of a particular community."

—*Dr. Martin Luther King, Jr.*

Morality is another thing that can never be replaced. In the choosing of my friends my mother used to voice this caveat; "you're either going to change them or they are going to change you!" It is one of the unspoken truths of any interpersonal relationship, we will either have impact upon those in our circle of influence or they will upon us. This effect can be either positive or negative, and the choice is ours to make. In an equitable or reciprocal relationship the choice is usually a good one and the damage (if any) is usually minimal or at least shared. In an imbalanced or abusive relationship however, the damages can be detrimental to say the least as one side gains all the benefits of the relationship while the other party is left with the proverbial "hind part" to kiss. These relationships have taken on many names over the years, particularly in the United States where its inability to treat all persons with justice and equality has blemished the quality of life for those of us who live here today. The Manifest Destiny doctrine as well as that of the Monroe Doctrine have proven to be nothing short of imperialism. Colonialism, and the American slavery that sustained them (a slavery much different than anything the world had ever seen,) were much worse. Jim Crow and the discriminatory attitudes that have prevailed since served to exacerbate these wounds, creating a bleeding that hasn't ceased since. Slavery and discrimination are more institutionalized now (and possibly more covert,) and its victims can't be confined strictly to the African American population in this country; a need for reform and *true Reconstruction* is on the horizon.

The truth is often a hard pill to swallow; our beloved Democracy isn't quite the amicable relationship it has been touted it to be. This representative democracy inundated with its lobbying and free enterprising isn't without its many failings. However, I do believe that the United States is still the best place **for me** to live. As a matter of fact, I cannot think of any other place that I might be afforded the opportunities I've been afforded. The writing of this essay itself is testament that this American edifice isn't some irrevocably condemned building, but a nation simply in need of *renovation.* I believe also that a resurgence of our founding principles must be brought to the forefront in order to keep our dilapidated structures from falling. Unfortunately, there is a self-righteousness that has accompanied our brand of democracy that has not allowed us to simultaneously behold both our splendor and manure. The more critical issue however, is our self-righteousness in the midst of moral depravity. This self-righteousness can be seen as nothing short of hypocrisy. This hypocrisy must be addressed if we are to progress as a nation. Our children look upon it with disdain, as do our adversaries around the world. We could really stand to "sweep around our own front doors," and to *remove the logs out of our own eyes* instead of worrying about *the splinters* of the rest of the world. How can the United States be a model and defender of the free world, when there are still pockets of our society that do not fully experience the freedoms enjoyed by our most privileged persons?

It is an oxymoronic notion that the United States (a country that in many respects is not free,) would be qualified to lead others to freedom. Saddam may not tyrannize our people but there is still tyranny in the land. Bombs do not fly overhead but many of our urban centers and impoverished cities are war zones. There are no official monarchs in the United States, but there are those who live as kings while others are treated worse than peasants. The rich have gotten richer while the poor have gotten poorer. Greed has overtaken philanthropy, and mutual cooperation has become nothing more than a "noble, utopian ideal." America needs to be *freed,* freed from the injustice, and hate, intolerance and selfishness that has been recycled throughout our history. We are bound within a moral vacuum; a moral debacle that has accelerated over the past thirty years. This has been a trend that all of America has shared. Though we are not the *"Melting Pot"* we proclaim to be, all of us (minorities and the majority alike,) have run this "rat race" called an *American Dream.* All of us as part of this American culture have bought into the idea that the essence of *"Life, Liberty and the Pursuit of Happiness"* can be summed up in a house on the hill, a six-figure job, a spouse and two and half kids. We have taken on a much less altruistic mindset than in generations past proclaiming that we will live life to the fullest (no matter what the cost,) and if we have to step on someone in the process then so be it. We justify our own greed by saying that the next man should simply be more industrious; and we justify our duplicity by simply saying *"you should do unto others before they do unto you."*

This new-aged hedonism isn't really new at all; it is seen in some of our most ancient and grand societies—*RIGHT BEFORE THEIR DEMISE*. We have chosen our own pleasures over the principles of God and individualism over community. I know personally that within my own race, we have regressed some way from the days of *We shall Overcome*, and even longer from *We Shall not be Moved*. Gone are the days of *I Hear Music in the Air, There must be a God Somewhere;* and as a nation even *We the People* doesn't have the same *Freedom Ring*. We have lost our way as those without a compass in a jungle of hate, and lasciviousness, selfishness, self-righteousness and pride. We are collectively lost and as a result we suffer LOSS everyday. We are losing on our streets and in our schools; in our homes, on our jobs, and even our sanctuaries where we claim to know God and His ways. We are losing, particularly in reference to the younger generations across this country who are quickly coming behind us. We pay millions of dollars to restore nightclubs in the name of redevelopment but we won't pay any money to rebuild a burned down church or a burnt out school system in the name of spiritual and educational renovation. We spend billions of dollars overseas to feed others while millions starve on the streets of this country everyday. We tax and overtax those who are poorer and in less of a financial position to pay taxes. Those who are more affluent however, benefit greatly from this Free Enterprise. They virtually get away *"scott free"* under a nuance we call the "tax break." Our Free Society isn't so free at all as it financially constrains and restrains families who don't want to get rich necessarily, but simply feed their families. There has to be more to life than working to earn just enough to barely pay your expenses. In a speech given by former Vice President Candidate John Edwards, he stated that "it is estimated that some 36 million people in the United States live in poverty; this includes women and children who work more than one job and still cannot afford housing." To make matters worse, the person who steals from *Wal-Mart* out of their necessity to eat can get a harsher penalty than someone who steals their employee's life savings and benefits, and we call it justice. It is possible for the child abused to receive a more severe penalty for murdering the child abuser (particularly if he or she is a 1st time offender.) We will call one a vigilante taking their life into their own hands and the other one an addict fighting back from a sickness. We are sick as a nation today, and if left untreated it will **become terminal**.

I have gathered some of the following statistics from a favorite site of mine powered by the Center for Moral Clarity:

- Some 44million abortions (larger than the populations of some countries) have occurred since 1973, erasing from the face of the earth potential Martin King's, Susan Anthony's, and Albert Einstein's before their lives really had a chance to begin.

93% of these of these abortions were not committed for reasons of rape or incest but simply because *childbearing and rearing wasn't as convenient as child making.* I call it TERMINAL ILLNESS.

- Pornography is an 8 billion dollar cash cow, while child pornography pulls in 3 billion. There are presumably just as many adult bookstores and video stores as there are McDonald's franchises; this gives new meaning to the McDonalds slogan where a little over 5 billion are served. (TERMINAL ILLNESS)
- How about the approximately 15million Americans who contract STD's annually and 8,219 new STD cases daily among teenagers, that is 342 an hour and 1 *every ten seconds.*

These are but a few of the factors that serve as evidence of what is to become a terminal illness if we do not reconsider our ways. We are a culture that does *what* it wants, *when* it wants, *how* it wants, *where* it wants and we call it liberality. This great nation, once a nation truly under God has chosen to divorce that same God; somehow forgetting that *there wasn't a United States before He brought us into being.* We slap God in the face with issues of blatant immorality and we slap God in the face with separation of church and state; a separation that somehow seeks to limit the church's influence in government but never the government's influence on the church. We slap God in the face with our lack of love and compassion, we slap God in the face with our greed and selfishness, our arrogance and deceit and finally, we slap Him the face when we try to assume His *"Godness"* as our very own. We really slap God when we try to hand down edict and judgment particularly upon those who believe differently as we, as if we were God ourselves. We are as an aggregate supposed to be a nation "in whom God we trust," it was our very first President who had the foresight to know that a job couldn't be performed without God and so he added the words "So help me God" to his (the very first) oath of office. His [God's] influence is inscribed within the halls of the Supreme Court itself (though at times you would hardly know it) as well as the Chambers of the House and Senate building. Even the dome of the Capitol itself shows veneration to Him and His relationship with us. His [God] foresight is reflected in our most valued and treasured documents and heard through the words of our most honored leaders of the times. And yet these voices from the past, these founding documents, this rich history and relationship with "the Creator" (as the Declaration of Independence declares) has largely faded away.

We must once again point ourselves in an upward direction. We must once again pull out our moral compasses and point to Him. We must point toward a path of progress and fulfillment. We must be able to better gauge between left and right and between good and bad. We as an American people (particularly those of African descent) should not want to "relive the old days," but it surely cannot hurt to seek the revival of old principles which has allowed us to enjoy the small amount of "success" we have experienced in the past. I caution against the excessively permissive culture that I see today. I caution against the unbridled relativity in which we deal with the moral, social and political issues of our day; I know we would like to think these issues are unrelated but they are. The power and benefit in liberality is not being able to do anything we want without regard just because all things were possible, but rather it is the ability to govern and even restrain one's self in the midst of a myriad of liberalities. Pop culture trends cannot be our guides; neither can music videos nor television shows be our compass. We must stand upon the **standard.** Our morality cannot be determined by the prevailing thought of the day, nor can it be determined by the whimsical desires or esoteric ideology that has no relevance in the earth; but by values that have sustained us throughout time. Honesty and integrity, perseverance, mutual respect and cooperation, unconditional love and discipline; these are the standards by which all of us (whether African American, Hispanic, Caucasian, Native American or whatever,) should live and be made of if we are to truly live in the image of God.

Article 5: A Need for Voice

○ ○
And God <u>said</u> "Let there be light AND THERE WAS LIGHT."

—Genesis 1:3

I have often thought to myself concerning God, *what a powerful voice*. What a voice one has to have to be able to bring illumination to the darkness of any condition; let my voice also bring light to the darkness of this sociopolitical landscape. The voice is by far (beyond any contraption or invention and beyond any weapon or tool,) the greatest and most powerful gift to man. In this American society alone, it is a most treasured commodity. We understand that in a democracy the majority *rules* because the vote of the majority elects. Therefore it is the voice of the majority that is always heard and who drives our public policies. Sometimes this majority is expressed in terms of sheer number as white America represents one majority; other times it is expressed in terms of who has the most capital as the rich and affluent represent another majority. In either case, those who are not in the majority are often the voices that go unheard; their voices become muffled even muted. The voices of the majority drowns out that of the minority, a pseudo-caste system begins to develop and the oppressed become disgruntled. The inequity in our society then manifests itself in more extreme attempts by minority voices to be heard. They are as small children who, when not *called on* in class have a proclivity to *call out, yell out or even scream*. Every time I watch the news or read the paper I see our youth (not only youth but people in general) all over our nation screaming and crying out. I see disenfranchised, disgruntled, and misguided people who are upset because they raised their hand and *nobody called on them*. I believe this is also the catalyst on an international scale behind terrorism; and while I do not agree with **the method** I can to some degree empathize with **the madness** that comes when no one is willing to hear what you have to say. Human beings deserve legitimacy, they deserved to be recognized for their ideas even if they are foreign to us.

We the people have fought hard just to have a voice. In the late 18th century there was the sentiment "no taxation without representation." Colonists were unwilling to be *taken from* by an oppressive British government without *being given back to*. Similarly, **We the people** as African Americans and Hispanics, Native Americans and Jewish, the poor and marginalized also deserve similar representation (voice.) Reciprocity from an America who was formerly an oppressor of many of the peoples I just named has to be the key. The majority must be more sensitive to the voices of those not like their own; conversely minorities must be more cognizant of the happenings around them and be willing to fight (be assertive) for their voice. It is a sin in my opinion to abuse, misuse, and underutilize they very same voice that many have bled and died for. In my own African American community (particularly in our urban centers,) our apathy and cynicism have stagnated our progress. As a nation at large we have passed that same cynicism to our children who in turn forfeit their own voice. As time passes and this condition worsens, ideas and innovations continue to go unseen and unheard.

I find it a bit eerie that we who pride ourselves with "free speech" are so quick to stifle the voices of those we don't want to hear. We stifle the voices of our own youth and in many of our own communities, we who were the oppressed have become the oppressor. In the African American community, we hurt ourselves. The same can of course be said for all of America, that when we turn our back on our youth we turn our back on ourselves; we cut off our own legs at the knees. Who else will walk us into tomorrow if not our young people? Young people, and other dissatisfied people in general do not speak up. They do not speak up because they are disappointed in an America that has reneged on too many promises. I personally can remember my dilemma early on in life as I pondered the many fallacies of American justice and inclusion. I thought about the hypocrisy of a Declaration of Independence that said *"We hold these truths to be self evident that all men are created equal, and are endowed by their Creator certain inalienable rights."* Authors who had or knew those who had slaves wrote the *Declaration of Independence*. They condoned (because of their refusal to abolish) the transport, the sale, the breeding, the beating and maiming, the murder, the rape, the hardships and the absolute abomination of slavery. Then there was the *Missouri Compromise*, and the *Emancipation Proclamation*—that only freed slaves in the rebellion states. Even after the war and *Reconstruction*, it was the *Hayes-Tilden Compromise* that removed all troops from the South sealing the fate of all African American people left behind in the South. The mayhem continued with Jim Crow policies of the South and the good old Christian brothers of the Ku Klux

Klan. Then there was the *Civil Rights movement* that brought on the deaths of great human beings such as John F. and Robert Kennedy as well as Malik Shabazz and Martin King. Just when I forget the atrocities of this nation against its African American brethren, I remember that the Native Americans were the first to suffer and that those Japanese internment camps were just as indefensible. When will we learn to "get along" and treat each other as equals? The future of our country cannot be disentangled from its unity (or ability to become unified.) Nor can our responsibility to lift our neighbor out of their misery be extricated from the notion of prosperity and affluence in this nation. If we don't seek to heal the divisive wounds of our nation we will experience yet another Civil War. We will not necessarily recreate the *physical war*, but a very real sociological war from which there will be no *Reconstruction*.

We have got to listen to each other's voices and those who are in the minority must be adamant about having their place "at the table or podium." Skepticism and cynicism does not give license to be non responsive. We can no longer be passive with our destiny but we must be participants in our destiny. *We have* got to vote, *we have* got to picket, *we have* got to march, *we have* got to rally, *we have* got to organize, and *we have* got to mobilize. *We have* got to persevere because future generations and the future of our world depend on our steadfastness. ***Unfortunately, what we have been doing is all wrong.*** We have taught our upcoming generations their apathy, we've taught them to stand upon the sidelines while taking credit for the win. We've not held up our end of the deal, we've not done a good job in raising them, and nurturing them and educating them. We have been derelict in serving as an example for our young people. We have not fought for them and been in their corner. We have been just as hypocritical as parents as our nation has been to the world. How can America fight wars of liberation abroad when there are those within its own border who have yet to be extricated from their oppression and affliction? We are guilty of not sweeping around our own front door; we have not raised and prepared our children (the next generation of Americans,) and we have not fully educated our people though we say no one is *left behind*. We haven't fed our families and demanded a stronger, more inclusive voice. We have instead blamed each other for not speaking loud enough, not being ambitious enough, and not having a desire to truly integrate into this system we have affectionately called the *American Way*. We have created an America of "haves" and "have nots;" of "insiders" and "outsiders." We have created disenfranchised, disgruntled people who express their disdain for their own "Land of the Free, and Home of the Brave." They express their anger in a brand of dysfunctional behavior, a domestic terrorism if you will; and whether it is the youth that carjacks you or the neo-nazi who openly proclaims revolution, even the Timothy McVeigh's of our country—one thing that is for certain is that they are unhappy with our current infrastructure. We had better learn to hear each other's voices.

We must teach our children to express their voice; in the African American community this is often so eloquently and powerfully portrayed in our music. Let us not only express our voice within our music, but also let it be felt in our voting and our speaking in public forums. I know that this is certain for my brothers and sisters in the African American community, and I'm sure that it can be generalized to my brothers and sisters abroad who feel disenfranchised and marginalized; if we voted more then perhaps Republicans wouldn't ignore us. If we voted more than maybe Democrats wouldn't give us lip service and take us for granted (as they consistently do with minorities and women.) If when given the opportunity, we stopped bickering with each other over the television and radio waves; if we spoke intelligibly then perhaps a coherent message could be communicated. I'm not advocating block voting nor am I shunning diversity in thought and practice, I am merely stating the need for there to be some things on which we *can* agree upon. There ought to be some core values on which we can all hinge our doors. The assumption that all African Americans, or all women, or all Republicans think alike is absurd; yet there ought to be some things as human beings that ought to be transcendent of all economic, cultural, religious, or political affiliations. For African Americans and minorities in general, there are external forces that still exist and that serve to impede them in their quest for equality. I also believe however, that our biggest problems are *not external but internal.* We all must work together in these struggles because if America is going to be successful abroad, America must finally deal with (and put to rest) its domestic inadequacies, inconsistencies and improprieties.

I am often grieved by what I witness in the urban school division in where I teach; where I see children fight more fiercely *against each other* only because they live in different neighborhoods than they do against a *system* that has relegated them to such a low standard of living. These neighborhoods though given different names are strikingly similar even down to the structural appearance of the apartments; (the same can be said about the *people* that live *within* those neighborhoods.) One would think that instead of fighting each other in an effort to ameliorate their frustration due to their condition that they would fight alongside each other to permanently revolutionize their condition. The same problem exists within America as a whole, as does my same conclusion. Instead of being in contention with and dispiriting each other, harassing and disparaging each other we need to fight alongside each other as *one voice*. One voice can be more easily heard and understood than many, differing and muffled ones. This is where leadership is integral. A leader simply directs the masses and shows the way to a desired destination. All of us as leaders have the responsibility to show someone else the way out of darkness into the light. There is power in numbers and power in the voice, and when we have ALL achieved justice and equality then we can rejoice. Let us learn to speak up and speak out, but more importantly let us also learn to listen to each other's voices.

Article 6: A Need for Leadership

○ ○

"The first into battle, the last to leave the job, the one who makes the greatest sacrifice, a servant of the people, a motivator, a guide, an example…This is a leader."

—Tony A. Harris, Jr.

The thirty second Kodak moments of life are nothing more than microcosms of larger real life truths. If we are watchful and attentive to the normalcy around us then we too will be able to see deep into the abyss of own social plight. We will be able to see things as they really are, both the dysfunction in its fullness as well as the appropriate solutions. I was recently in the elementary school where I now work when I had a memorable Kodak encounter with a young man who couldn't have been more than six or seven years old. I met him in a bathroom, as I walked in he was already there—he'd climbed on the sink in an effort to wash his hands. I watched him briefly run water over his hands and as a lot of young people didn't bother to use soap. I came over alongside him, said hello and began to wash my own hands. He watched intently as I vigorously lathered my hands and then washed. In a second effort the young man climbed upon the sink again, and washed his hands again. This time he too began to lather his hands and wash in the same fashion he had watched me. As we shared a smile and I opened the door for him, I stopped and pondered what had just taken place. It was at that moment that I finally understood the importance of leadership. Leadership is a lost art in our American culture, and so the question that arises for me is *"why?"* Where are leaders who possess the patriarchic caliber of our early heroes such as Washington, or Jefferson? Who among us instead of placating the few is willing to make the tough decisions for the whole like Lincoln? Who has the courage of a Harriet Tubman, the forthrightness of a Malik Shabazz, the charisma of a John F. Kennedy or the vision of a Martin Luther King? Where have our leaders gone, have not our circumstances called for them to rise again? Where will our young people look to in the absence (or rather *who* will they look to?) It reminds me of a passage I meditate on from the bible that reads:

> *Jesus went through all the towns and villages teaching in the synagogue, and preaching the good news of the kingdom, and healing every disease and sickness. When he saw the crowds he had compassion on them because they were harassed and helpless, like a sheep without a shepherd. Then he said to his disciples, "the harvest is plentiful but the workers are few. Ask the Lord of the harvest therefore to send out workers into the harvest field. [Matthew. 9:35-38, NIV]"*

Where are the leaders that proclaim the *good news* unto the masses? Where are those who stand in the forefront, serving as *agents of healing?* Where are the men and women of compassion for the people, who see this nation and this world in a state of confusion and instability? I have prayed for God to send them and so should you.

There is so much work to be done. There are so many voices to be heard, persons to be served and uplifted, and injustices to be fought against (the list goes on and on.) Yet there are so few who would stand in the gap to meet the need and the challenges that we face as an American people. Brother and Sisters of all shades, creed, ethnicity, we need a few good men, women, and children of integrity. We need persons who will be honest not just because *big brother is watching*, but because that's just the essence of whom they are. We need those who are willing to lead with a persona that suggests that they are not above the people, but in the midst of the people and accountable to the people. We need selfless individuals who understand that the benefits of the plurality outweigh the desires of one (or even a handful.) We need leadership who won't live their life to the fullest while others around them die, but those leaders who are willing to live or die themselves that others may attain a better life. There has been little progress in the annals of history without leaders. At the forefront of every moment in our history there have been great leaders. They were those who served as embers keeping the fire burning; it was they who served as the impetus for social upheaval and justice. They were our guiding lights, they showed their fellowman how to live and that change is sometimes necessary. As I make an assessment of the state of affairs in all of our separate sub communities (Asian, African American, Hispanic, etc) and the collective American community in which we live; I can only conclude that the stagnation experienced in them are not the faults of "apathetic" youth. Our issues are instead a direct byproduct of those who have absented themselves from leadership; leaving those same young people devoid of both direction and purpose. One of biggest fallacies is that leadership is not welcomed, particularly among the next generation. We believe for some reason that "other" people's needs are radically different from our own, and that leadership isn't easily accepted. The truth of the matter regarding our young people is that they *do want* our leadership, and that they *will respect* our leadership. Our young people are not ambivalent to our voices nor are they apathetic to our concern; they are simply leery of our *new age post 1970 lip service leadership*. This is a leadership of empty promises, a leadership that *talks the talk* but is unable to *walk the walk*. One thing I have noticed about our young people are that they are very good judges of character. They can "see you coming a mile away;" they detect the disingenuous and they have very low tolerance for hypocrisy. America deserves substantive leadership; a leadership not composed of simply the shell, but of the egg white and the yoke as well. Great movements necessitate leaders, and leaders cultivate great movements; *and we are in the need of both right now.*

What is a ship without its captain, conversely what is a captain without a ship? How about an army without a general, or a general without an army? Both must go hand and hand, *message and messenger*, otherwise you are left with a force without direction. We might be strong but we will never hit our target or reach our destination without leadership. Leaders inspire and challenge their followers to action; they challenge them to ascend to a higher standard of living. Leaders also *reproduce themselves*, meaning they duplicate leaders who will lead in their stead and pick up where they left off. Leaders leave behind a legacy, a new paradigm for humanity that lives on even after they themselves have died.

If we had true leaders then we would not so easily accept the notion that athletes and entertainers are sound role models, particularly since leadership in that regard is not a role many of them welcome. The argument of the "Charles Barkley's" of the world is not one I necessarily agree with (for whom much is given, much is also required.) However, we all must consider that perhaps it is not wise to call on those to lead who wish not to lead. Too often these leadership mantles are inappropriately placed upon persons because of their popularity or affluence and not because of their leadership *calling*. One thing I know about positive leadership is that leaders do not abdicate responsibility; even if they delegate responsibility they know the "buck stops" with them. They understand the weight of their mantle as well as the authenticity of their calling and they don't back down. They do not complain that there are those who are depending on them and those who look up to them. While many true leaders do not profess perfection they are cognizant of the implications of their influence upon the masses and live accordingly. I know that within my own African American community, I tire of seeing these so called "models of blackness;" these so-called African American ambassadors who resemble a Barnum and Bailey Circus more so than they do the community. They do not provide the leadership for our young Black nation, nor do they instill the pride in them necessary for them to grow. What they do however is stand on public platforms and spout out a few of our issues (pleasing themselves with the media coverage,) and then retreat back to their comfort zones. They spend more time on their make up and their speech preparation than they do working toward a sound solution. As a collective our country faces the same dilemma, leaders who look like leaders but are not; their value solely cosmetic. Will the real leadership of this nation please stand up? I'm not talking about those who would make sure that every year they passed a law for their own pay increase, while not being able to agree on a balanced budget for everyone else; nor am I talking about those who'll stop everything to have hearings on a certain spectator sport, while at the same time not being able to ensure healthcare for all. What I am talking about is *leadership that brings a new vitality to a swiftly decomposing society*. What we have recently been experiencing in terms of leadership can be likened to a child on a junk food diet of chips, and cookies, doughnuts, and candy (it is NO WONDER we have such upset stomachs!) What the child is in need of is a *healthy and balanced* diet; a diet of vegetables and meat, bread, fruit and so on. A diet such as this is sure to produce healthy and strong children, and so I offer the same prescription for a malnourished America: **real leadership**. We need leadership that exists in our homes, in the Church, in our communities, and on both the national and international stage.

Article 7:
A Need for Achievement

"Probably one of the most serious psychological handicaps young people have today is the notion that is it cool to be a non-achiever, that it is hip to put down hard work in school."

—Dr. Bill Cosby

One thing is certain; leaders sometimes must be candid and forthright in their assessments of the people they lead as well as the institutions that oppose them. One cannot deny the impediments faced as a woman, a minority, or as one of less affluence in this country; however, if you check our history you will see that impediments while a hindrance, are no excuse for failure. To achieve means *to perform* or *carry out with success*, it means *to attain* with effort *despite difficulty*. It is time to bring America back to place of achievement.

I can remember a story I heard from a man who was born in the generation before mine. He (unlike myself,) had to deal with the atrocities of segregation and then forced integration. We have spent moments from time to time discussing the direction both of this nation and of our African American people during the span of our lifetimes; it is amazing sometimes to note that while there is a thirty-year age and experiential difference between us there are some things that never change.

He once told me the story of how he came up in the projects of Richmond, Va. He told of how he persevered from such a meager beginning to go to college, and then onward to receive his Doctorate. He began his story with Christmas one year where he received three gifts: a piece of fruit, one toy, and a pocket dictionary. The fruit, he said was eaten by lunchtime; the toy broken by evening but the dictionary lasted him a lifetime. His mother, who did not have the same educational opportunities that many of us enjoy today, mandated him to memorize one word each day. In addition to memorizing that word he was also instructed to both learn the correct pronunciation and use the word in a sentence. She told him never to lose the dictionary, and if he did to never come home (an admonishment he took literally.) Everyday her procedure would be to ask her son upon his arrival home what his word was for that particular day. This was the arrangement until one day he noticed the *fellas out on the corner* laughing at him and calling all sorts of names. Ironically, it was some of the same derogatory verbiage I hear children use to insult each other today; words such *faggot, punk,* or *sissy.* This was naturally disconcerting as the young African American male found himself negatively influenced by peer pressure. He hid *his gift* in the bushes and was immediately accepted by he friends. He began to play basketball until it began to rain, but in his rush home he inadvertently left the dictionary in the bushes. As he walked into the door his mother began their usual ritual and *she asked him for his word.* His palms began to perspire and his heart rate quickened because he knew he had left his book. Not knowing how to proceed he spouted the first word that came to mind; POISE. "Poise" he said, "to remain calm under pressure." His mother looked at him strangely, went to her room and pulled out a notebook that she had. In her notebook she had recorded (unbeknownst to him) ALL OF HIS WORDS, and it would seem that he'd used that very same word two weeks prior! He tried his best to justify himself sharing with his mother the names of all the other boys in the neighborhood whose mothers were not so hard on them. She retorted what has been proclaimed for ages by parents of all ages, shapes, and sizes; "those aren't my children, YOU ARE." She told him to go back into the rain, and find that dictionary. She told him *that those teachers at that school* may not think anything about him, but *she did* (and yes he did get the beating of his life!)

Many of us who are different often do as this young man did; we hide our gifts that we might be accepted by those around us. By diluting ourselves we only shortchange ourselves; denying the potential that is so deep within us. We behave as one who sits in the dark refusing to simply "flick the switch." What good is the light if you never turn it on? The impact of this mother's love wouldn't be felt until sometime later when one of the young man's teachers (admiring his elocution and command of the English language,) asked him about his upbringing. When he told her that he lived in the projects adjacent to the school and that his parents were not doctors or lawyers but blue-collar workers, she simply could not believe it. She could not fathom someone from such marginal beginnings being able to transcend circumstance and achieve so much. His mother who did not even have a high school education, **expected more** from him than a teacher with a college degree.

Expectation and achievement go hand in hand; if you cannot see it, then it cannot be done. This is an issue very dear to my heart as an educator in an inner city. For too long, we have declined in our achievement because it has been deemed "not cool." We have allowed ourselves to drift into the abyss of academic deficiency because we were not expected to achieve. All I can say to that notion is that *"the devil is a liar,"* we have always been achievers and innovators. There is a pattern and a precedent of and for achievement. As one reads from the pages of Dr. Jawanza Kunjufu's *Lessons from History: A Celebration in Blackness*, one finds that the first universities were African, the Grand Lodge of Wa'at and the University of Timbuktu. Math, science, history and religion all have their origins in Africa. The notion of monotheism embraced by the three major religions of the world (Christianity, Judaism, and Islam,) can also be recognized in ancient African culture. All of the profound philosophers recognized by our American culture: Socrates, Hippocrates, Aristotle, and Plato were influenced by the genius of African culture. It is possible that they were not only influenced, but that they stole the culture of Africa and took it as their own. George James further illustrates these points in a book entitled *Stolen Legacy*. A lot of us do not know these truths and yet, this isn't a hard concept to grasp given our own American history. We observe an American history where slaves who couldn't afford to buy patents (or weren't allowed,) forfeited the credit of their genius to their masters. Even today a certain degree of genius in the realm of music, and clothing, our swagger and our culture has been emulated but not properly accredited. We are as a subculture often outwardly despised yet inwardly envied. What is even more shameful is that African American people as whole do not seem to see what others see. It would seem that everybody (and I do not say it in an egotistical manner,) wants to be us BUT US. Our hands were among the first to realize the reality of open-heart surgery as well as the successful separation of Siamese twins adjoined at the back of the head. We were integral in the construction of the capital of this country (Washington, D.C.,) and some of its most beloved structures including the Capitol building itself. We made the transatlantic journey to the Americas 3,000 years before Columbus and *well before* being accosted to partake of the Middle Passage; In other words, there is quite simply no rational or logical reason for underachievement. I speak of these things not to promote racial exclusivity or superiority *of any kind* in this nation, but to instill a pride in a race within this nation who have forgotten who they are.

I am firm believer that one cannot free others without first being free. I cannot imagine the full liberation of this nation without first seeing the freedom of the community from which I come. As I have presented throughout these essays however, the problems (*needs*) inherent in African American community are not exclusive to our community. These issues are a microcosm of the issues that cancerously malign the nation. What effects one has impact on us all and no one is truly free unless all of us are free. Anyone who ignores this fact lives under the false impression that there is such a thing as isolationism and they falsely assume that the sins and maladies of another will never come knocking at their door. But the real truth of the matter is that it already has and has been doing so for quite some time. As I look at an article written by Marc A. Fey in June 2003, I see some startling statistics concerning education in America. It reads that while America has nearly doubled its expenditures on education in the past thirty years, its quality continues to decline. The article continues to state that according to a test given in 1995, American 12th graders rank 19th out of 21 countries in the areas of math and science. According to this same article, an assessment given in 2000 showed that only 32 percent of 4th graders were proficient in reading, 29 percent in writing and 26 and 18 percent respectively in math and science (these children are currently in middle and high school all across our country.) How's that for "No Child Left behind?"

We should expect more of ourselves. We need to **require** our young people (this next generation,) to achieve. And while much of the general public support holding schools and educators directly accountable for student achievement (or lack of,) there is our own negligence to consider. We need to teach our young people to expect a lot more from each other as well. It should not be *cool* to be *dumb*, what kind of friend celebrates another friend's foolishness? We all could stand to push each other to do better. There was a time when kids (the majority of them,) competed for better grades. We knew that in order to get ahead you had to work *harder* than the next person (not simply *just as hard*.) We used to know that this world owed us nothing and that we had to earn everything we had. Conversely, our youth today (along with the rest of contemporary America) believe that the world owes them something and that they are entitled to all things. We used to be aspired to be the best we could be: doctors, lawyers, engineers, politician, and teachers; now we are only concerned with what can get us from 0 to 60mph in under six seconds. We used to follow our passions notwithstanding the pay, and now our only passion is the pay.

I am concerned (particularly with some of those in African American communities,) who advocate this "pipe dream" that relegates our youth *strictly* to athletics and/or entertainment. This often facilitates a *"dumbing down"* of the community if you will, particularly among the males. This isn't so much the case with our women who do not enjoy the same revenue potential in athletics at the professional level. As a result, females continue to excel academically at a higher rate than do our males. There is nothing wrong with a profession in entertainment, or athletics; *but only a handful of us were* given the God-given talent to pursue such a dream, and *an even smaller handful of them* will ever live to see such a dream materialize. Fortunately, history proves that these areas (athletics and entertainment,) are not the only areas of our strength; as a matter of fact these are merely recent blips on our radar screen. African American contributions span the globe and are not confined to the North American and African continents. Europe continued to believe the earth was flat until the Moors came into Italy and Spain offering a different experience; it was no doubt an influential factor for Christopher Columbus and the Spanish Government who financed his expedition. The central question remains however, **what have we done lately?** What has African America done lately? What pyramids have they erected in this age? We have seen the glory of Sumeria, Songhay, Mali, Ghana, Carthage, Ethiopia, and Egypt spanning over 5,000 years but what shall we do in America as African Americans today? What shall America do itself? We no longer live in the days of Post WWI where America emerged a the "new kid on the block." Nor do we live in the WWII era, of which produced what has often been called the "Greatest Generation" in American History. The Communist threat might be a thing of the past, we might be the lone superpower of the world but we are not alone. The world has quickly caught up (and in some cases surpassed,) these United States of America all because we have rested upon our laurels and ceased to achieve.

Once again I contend that this is a universal need in our country today. Our young people will not gain our perspective through osmosis, but instead they must be re-taught. They must be inspired and supported and encouraged. They must not "hide their gifts in bushes" for fear that we will shun them. We must think more of them even when the people around them (even when they themselves,) do not. I firmly believe that the impetus for achievement must be rooted in education. It was Malcolm X who was quoted as saying that *"**Education is an important element in the struggle for human rights. It is the means to help our children and our people rediscover their identity thereby increasing self-respect. Education is the passport for the future, for tomorrow belongs to those who plan for it today.**"*

Everyone's path will not be the same, but all of us require **a path** to his or her greatness (there are no shortcuts.) *Everyone will not receive a college degree but* *everyone should be educated and knowledgeable in whatever they choose to do*; **igno-rance is not bliss**. Man's (or woman's) life is always confronted with questions, and they are forever set out on a quest to answer those questions. Education is about answering those most basic questions. The cultures of northern and western Africa were examples of education at its finest, as was ancient Rome and Greece. Man will stop at nothing to seek such education; men have always known the power in it. Slaves were whipped, blinded, and maimed just for attempting to gain understanding. African Americans in the early and late twentieth century erected colleges and universities of their own all over the country because they were not allowed higher education anywhere else. They understood the value of education and it's inextricable link with achievement. For many of us who have made it out, it was the only way out; it was the door to a better tomorrow. We must now re-open that door, all of our children must be encouraged to achieve. We either rise as a collective people or we do not rise at all. In the end, we can only be as strong as that weakest link: ACHIEVEMENT

Article 8: A Need for Resources

o o o o o o o o o o o o o o o o o o o o o o o o o o o o o o o o o

*"There are resources all around us everyday, most of us however aren't **resourceful** enough to find them. These resources pale in comparison to those within us, and unfortunately most of us take far too long to find them; too."*

—*Tony Avon Harris, Jr.*

What ever happened to the old cliché, "If you want the job done right, do it yourself? Whatever happened to self sufficiency and being able to do all things well? I am not talking about being a "jack of all trades but excellent at none;" what I am suggesting is balance and a well roundedness that comes from having tried all things and persevering until one is at least proficient at one of them. It is impossible to be an *expert* at everything, but it is very possible to at least be good at many things; the more you are good at, the less someone else has to be good *for* you. In this world of interdependence and the connectedness of humankind, isolationism (as I have already mentioned) is not a realistic or healthy idea. However, one can become so dependent on the services of another that those services become indispensable and so numerous that one does absolutely nothing for themselves. In business this practice is known as *outsourcing*.

Consider the analogy about Company Y; they contract (outsource) so many other companies to do their work for them that they (Company Y) do nothing for themselves. There are three ramifications for such a practice.

1. **It's hard to keep a pulse on the day-to-day operation** if you are not directly involved (abdicating responsibility is never good.)

2. **It always costs *something* to outsource** (even if you don't see the price today, it is money you could be saving or allocating to some other area of need.)

3. **Outsourcing creates an environment of taking without giving.**
    When you are taking without any intention or ability to give back, you
    will either (a) become dispensable yourself because you offer little or (b)
    become a threat by depleting the services and ability of those you draw
    from (you take a lot.)

You can peruse the internet and find as I found on the www.cnn.com/Lou
Dobb's featured site that a lot of American companies outsource; from *Aetna* to
Amazon. COM, from *Bank of American* to *Dupont*, even heavyweights like *Halliburton*, *Hewlett Packer*, and *Yahoo* do business overseas. However, it is a practice
that is frowned upon by certain parties because it is said to take away jobs from
home. While outsourcing seems to save money in an immediate sense (as well as
offer tax breaks,) the long-term effects are detrimental. The outsourcing that I am
talking about however is not one of business practice; rather it is the *outsourcing*
of our greatest **resource:** *people*. The practice I speak of has more broad sweeping
implications than any practice of the companies just mentioned, because it is not
jobs lost, but souls lost. We export the soul of our communities and nation
because we have engaged in this practice for so long. We now find ourselves
depleted and in a position where we need not to outsource, but to find resources.

Perhaps you did not notice but America is paying the price for its outsourcing.
We have outsourced our rights and responsibilities as a culture. This is shown in
the least of things such as voting where less than half of the nations eligible voters
actually participate in that facet of the political process. It is also shown in the
way we rear (or rather allow someone or something else to rear) our children. We
have outsourced life itself and happily accepted the raw end of the deal. Those we
have outsourced to have taken our money and run. They have offered an inferior
product, hardly comparable to what we have within our own capabilities. In
everything from education to employment and from our finances to our dreams
we have allowed others to give us cheap imitations of our own potential (AND
WE PAY THEM FOR IT.) It would seem that if we do not *have* to do a thing,
more than likely *we do not*. Is their something about *upward mobility* that says the
less you have to do for yourself, the better off you are? The time is now for us
to choose from our own resource pools to do the things we need to do as individual communities and as a nation.

Who told us that we could not make it on our own, and who told us that we
needed their help? Assistance from anyone who would abuse and misuse you isn't
help at all; it is exploitation. In my own community for many of my twenty nine
years I have watched us struggle because we had not learned as a people to stick

together and support each other. We did not have to outsource because we were a wealth of resources in and of ourselves. Deep within us (as African Americans and Americans as a whole,) lies unlimited capability. There is absolutely nothing that we ca not do as *"We the people."* We have not been bystanders but participants on the world stage; we have just as much to be proud and thankful for as anybody else. But to ensure continued participation, and achievement on the world stage we have to return to the care of our greatest resource; our children. Our young as we have discussed, are being squandered at a rate analogous to that of petroleum, coal, or land. Are they not as precious and natural a resource as any of those? Do not the consequences of dereliction of such a resource (our children) prove to be as equally catastrophic? If we pollute the waters, we won't have anything to drink; and if we destroy the ozone and the air, we won't have anything to breathe. If we exhaust all of our petroleum and fossil fuel reserves then we lose major sources of energy and doom all of humanity to a cold and dark future; environmentalists know this very well. I am surprised however, that many of us are not as well informed as to what will happen if we don't prepare this next generation of Americans for tomorrow, this is the war we can't afford to lose. Do we not notice the subtle extinction extending from the ghettoes to the suburbs? Death (whether literal or figurative) does not discriminate based on color, or gender (though males seem to be the preferred target,) socioeconomic status or religious affilia-tion. This continuing spiritual and moral debacle continues yet no one is step-ping in with the urgency and attention this matter deserves; have not we figured it out that *if they die we die?* As the dreams of little African American boys and girls fade along with the dreams of little white boys and girls, and Hispanic girls and boys, Asian and Native American boys and girls, we must realize that so does the vision for this new nation fade. As their blood spills in the streets so does the life force of this country drain into the gutters and alleys of despair; down a road of *"would've beens, should've beens, and could've beens."*

We must understand that this is not just a matter of unrealized potential, we are not just missing out on a surplus of new ideas; rather we suffer a deficit as a result of the loss of each young person. We lose ideas, concepts, and dreams; all of which are integral to the survival of a nation in one way or another. At this rate, we are making a ton of withdrawals in this nation without any deposits on the horizon. How long will it be before our bank statement reads INSUFFICIENT FUNDS? It is when funds are insufficient that we outsource (seek others sources,) and borrow from others what we should have on our own. This is the situation America finds itself in on many levels both literally and figuratively. The jobs intended for us are overseas, the brilliance formerly ours was seized by others who were hard working enough to take our place, even the families and communities we were given stewardship over have been *given away* and *handed over* to anyone who will take the job. Our televisions and movie stars spend more time with our futures (our children) than we do. We have a debt so huge we will never pay it back; I have even heard we owe the United Nations money! (This is ironic since we spend billions in aid to many of the countries of the world.) We have put ourselves in a position where we borrow at a rate that is not equitable with our capacity to repay, and now we have developed bad credit. *Poor credibility* among the nations of the world, poor credibility among the people *within the nation*! There are people in our own country who would commit terrorist acts against it, what kind of sickness do we have if we would shoot ourselves in the leg? We are in such a predicament because on all levels in America there is too much taking, and not enough mutual giving; too many *imports* not enough *exports*. We stick our hands out to borrow more than we extend our hands to contribute. I also see this same vice at work within the African American community where we buy from everybody else except from our own people and where we will help anybody but ourselves. America has got to wake up and take inventory of the many resources in the diversity of people that it has within itself. If we continue with our current practices, we will find ourselves in a continued state of dependency and bondage. All of us in America are living below our calling, living below both the glory of our past and the potential of our future. My message to my African American brothers and sisters is the same message I convey to all of my American brothers and sisters alike:

We are not those considered the tail, but those considered the head. We are heads of households, heads of companies and heads of state. We are not borrowers but lenders because we are an American nation of resourcefulness. Now let's use it before we lose it!

Conclusion:
A Need for Growth and Change

o o o o o o o o o o o o o o o o o o o o o o o o o o o o o o o o o o o

"Growth is ALWAYS a difficult thing, but at the same time it is a necessary thing. It requires one to occupy more space than he or she previously did (spiritually, mentally, or physically.) Growth requires a stretching of some sort (and very few of us like to be STRETCHED,) that in turn causes growing pains. The only option to growth however is stagnation which is equivalent to death."

—*Tony Avon Harris, Jr.*

There was a saying I heard from Coach Pat Riley on ESPN's *Sportscentury* that seems so poignant for our conversation; He said, "Until you change the way you look at things, the things you look at will never change." We have become anesthetized by our own stagnation. Knowing the issues that confront us are one thing and hypothesizing a course of action is even better; however, the time has truly come for us to move out of the theoretical vacuum we call knowledge and idealism into the praxis we call reality. Let's stop the talk about progress in America and start walking in it. Particularly for the people of God (one nation under God,) it is time for us to initiate the movement, to part the walls of the sea instead of merely riding the tide. The key to our survival is not the *anticipation* of a brighter day, but *application* of the fundamental principles of freedom, equality, and God that the country was built upon. America was able to overcome the stain of **oppression** left by the acrimonious treatment of slaves by their slave masters. Millions of Africans were enslaved and murdered, their blood on the hands of an America who wanted nothing more than free labor. History has an ironic way of requital as America itself was almost destroyed over what *eventually* became an issue of slavery. The end of that war brought an end to the oppression that marred this country but it could not discourage the **segregation** that ensued. We fooled ourselves into believing that racial harmony would somehow be promoted by racial separation. For some reason we actually believed that separate could be equal. Separate however, would never be equal and our separation ensured that we would never interact long enough to have harmony. Differences in understanding exacerbated differences in treatment and the war for *Civil Rights* proved to be a civil war revisited. The laws changed but hearts did not; and where segregation was no longer defensible by law, **discrimination** was not as easily legislated. Affirmative action was a half-hearted attempt to make it better (and something is surely better than nothing,) yet we still have a long way to go in America. Third time was not the charm as we fight on yet another plateau, stretching ourselves a little farther that we might be a more civilized society and model of the free world. The war we fight today is not one of brown people vs. white people, or red people vs. yellow people or anything of the sort; the color of contention today is *green.* We fight a battle of economic inequality in what I call **institutional destitution.** The rich get richer while the poor are held under a ceiling and a system that perpetuates their poverty. According to David Levine, an economist at the University of California, Berkeley: "Being born in the elite in the U.S. gives you a constellation of privileges that very few people in the world have ever experience. Being born poor in the U. S. gives you disadvantages unlike anything in Western Europe and Japan and Canada." Racism is a volatile climate but classism is enough to solicit revolution. When the gap between those who "have," and those who "have not" widen, trouble looms on the horizon. Can't you see the frustration in the eyes of our youth and disenfranchised? The system does not work for them and so they seek ways *outside* of that system.

The only way to conquer this demon is through unity. There is a passage in the bible which states that *"a house divided against itself cannot stand."* We can no longer afford to play the race wars and class wars; we must be on one accord. We must all be as committed to making life better for our fellowman or women as we are for ourselves. The youth in this nation (and marginalized people along with them,) feel hopeless in the current system. These people have seen and felt the residual effects of this nation's greed, hypocrisy, and loveless practices. They have heard the vain words, and seen the half-hearted action, and they do not want any part of it. When we look on the corners and in the streets we are looking at those who did not fit into an exclusive system. When we find ourselves confronted with people who are out of control (and who exist under a different code of self control,) we have no one to blame but ourselves. We should not look any farther than the mirror; America's decadence did not begin yesterday but has evolved over time with its refusal to live out the tenets that are expressed on its very founding documents.

Our sins have truly come back to haunt us. Both at home and abroad the hatred and exploitation we have sown along with the prejudice shown and wrongs refused to be made right have shown up at our front door in all manner of evil. Our drugs, our alcoholism, our weapons, our overall selfishness and lasciviousness have left our children susceptible to the madness we call normalcy in the modern world.

The good news is however, that just as *we were* responsible for yesterday and today *we are also* responsible for today and tomorrow. We must not only be educated concerning the afflictions and needs of the next generation but we must be educated of their need and our need for *Mobilization, Identity, Hope, Moral Integrity, Voice, Leadership, Achievement and Resources.* We must allow that education to instill in us a certain *consciousness and a conscience.* A consciousness and a conscience that moves from empathy to participation; a consciousness that allows each other to see ourselves for who we really are. We are all brothers and sisters in this country; we are all brothers and sisters in this world. We initially share the same origin as humankind and we will ultimately share the same eschaton. This United States and the world for that matter is a part of one vast human community. This community is much bigger than race or class; it is much bigger than we could ever imagine and if we are going to win this *real* war then it is going to have to be done with all of us working together. We cannot afford to *"leave people behind"* as we so affectionately say in the field of education; but we have to open up the dialogue and hear each other's voices. If revival or reform is ever to take place we must first wake up to the reality and conditions that the oppressed, discouraged and marginalized face. We have to put our heads together and work together to prosper together because we can never *truly* live apart. Consider the power of **concentration**. Light *dispersed* offers only a few bright spots while *concentrated* light becomes a mighty laser able to slice through steel. Water is another example as water dispersed will only do minor cleansing and moistening. The same water dispersed in a concentrated form will over time erode the concrete structures of injustice; that same concentrated water will wash all remnant of sin away like a tidal wave going through the valley. We are the lights of this world with living water flowing from our bellies, and we have got to take our world back.

This is a war we can't afford to lose; this is a war for the world and the generations of tomorrow. I appeal to all who would to fight and to choose their weapons wisely. Every shot counts and every enemy destroyed is one less that can prey upon our people. I pray for each of us as each one of us plays our part to bring peace in this country and on the earth. I know that I will never meet some of you who read these essays, and I also know that I may not live to see the seeds of this work come into fruition. I do however; know that anything that any of us can do to help somebody else is a worthwhile venture. I look at myself in my own profession as a teacher where I have both good days and bad days. It is not always easy to present materials in a fashion that I palatable for today's young minds. Some days you "hit the ball out of the park," other days you "strike out." Some days I feel that the apathy of our young is a hill too insurmountable to climb, but I press on with the hope that I would reach *just one* child. Some of us like students in a class are pliable, ready and eager for growth while others sit with their heads on their desks feeling frustrated and self defeated. We are a mixed classroom in America; an amalgam of personalities, passions, talents, and experience. The key is commitment to the achievement of the class as a whole and not just certain individual students. We all have stake in this country and we all will excel if we continue to help each other, building bridges to and from each other in order to create a web of interdependence and love. It is all about building that bridge from each other into tomorrow.

I remember recently watching one of my more challenging students the other day as he stood on the other side of the glass window looking into my class. He had been kicked out his other class and he had somehow matriculated down the hall and found his way to my front door. As he peered into the window watching the class work I could see his frustration; I could see in his teary eyes his desire to be apart of the program despite his behavioral inability to conform. I too; was frustrated because I wanted very much for him to be apart of the program, yet I didn't have the capacity (at that moment,) to help him in. He as a result, could not come to where we were, and we could not go back to where he was. I purposed in my heart that day that I was going to do an even better job at being a bridge. I am going to be a bridge for those who find themselves "on the outside looking in," those "kicked out of the system." Why? Because I firmly believe that there is room at the table for EVERYBODY. You never know, the person you allow to the table today may be the one *feeding you tomorrow.*

I thank God for the ability to use what weapons (my words) I have for the betterment of people. Words for me are the most powerful vehicles on this planet; they are able to take you places that you could never travel by car, train, or plane. Words are both temporal and spatial agents, able to transcend both time and space. They are able to fight the battles that cannot be won by fists, or guns, or bombs. May my written words be internalized and hidden deep within the hearts of men, women, boys and girls; and may those same words be externalized into activity that makes this world a better place for all of our children to live. Thank you for considering my *Perspectives on the Real War*.

About the Author

Tony A. Harris, Jr. is an author, an alternative education instructor of at risk middle school aged children and an advocate for social justice. He is founder and devoted Pastor of True Vine Fellowship Ministries headquartered in Richmond, Virginia. Tony currently resides in a county of Richmond with his wife Najiyyah. He encourages readers to contact him at info@truevinefellowshipministries.org.

AUTHOR CONTACT INFORMATION

Tony Harris is available for lectures, various speaking engagements and book signings. Please contact his office staff at:

Tony A. Harris, Jr.
P. O. Box 5734
Midlothian, Virginia 23112
804-897-6254—office
804-683-4280—mobile office
804-897-6215—fax
www.truevinefellowshipministries.org
www.truevinetreasures.com

Perspectives on the Real War: Essays of a Human Condition in Crisis is also available on Audio Book. This eight CD package is available for $25.00 (U.S.) Please visit www.truevinetreasures.com for details.

Topics from *Perspectives on the Real War: Essays of a Human Condition in Crisis* may be heard on *True Vine Treasures* the daily/weekly radio ministry of True Vine Fellowship Ministries. *True Vine Treasures* may be heard in 18 eastern states and 6 Canadian provinces. For radio station details please visit www.truevinetreasures.com

978-0-595-38038-1
0-595-38038-7